The Spiritual Aspects
of
Psychiatric Practice

Also by Paul R. Fleischman, M.D.

The Healing Spirit

The Spiritual Aspects
of
Psychiatric Practice

Paul R. Fleischman, M.D.

BONNE CHANCE PRESS

Portions of this book were presented at the 149th Annual Meeting of the American Psychiatric Association on May 26, 1993, in San Francisco and will soon be available on audiocassette. Write the publisher for more information.

Printed in the United States of America

FIRST EDITION

The text of this book is composed in Times New Roman and the display type is set in Arial and Ellensburg. Book design by Sue Chance, M.D.

ISBN 0-9638398-2-9

1 2 3 4 5 6 7 8 9 0

For
William N. Grosch, M.D., M.Div.
in gratitude for
your broad appreciation
of human nature, and
your skill in bridge building

Contents

The Oskar Pfister Award Lecture of the American Psychiatric Association

The American Psychiatric Association annually presents an Oskar Pfister Award to a person who has made "important contributions to the humanistic and spiritual side of psychiatric issues." The award, consisting of an invited lecture and an honorarium, is named after a Swiss clergyman who maintained a lifelong relationship with Freud, and who has come to symbolize the potential cross-pollination of psychiatry and religion. The intention of the award is twofold: "To honor an outstanding contributor in the field of psychiatry and religion"; and "To broaden the base of issues addressed at the American Psychiatric Association's annual meeting by highlighting the role of humanity in complementing science."

Previous Oskar Pfister Award winners include neurologist Oliver Sacks, historian Peter Gay, theologian Hans Küng, and Auschwitz survivor and existentialist psychiatrist Viktor Frankl. Because the Award is also given to individuals from other countries and other disciplines, only five American psychiatrists have been chosen: Jerome Frank, Robert J. Lifton, Robert Coles, William Meissner, and Paul Fleischman.

Selections from this essay, "The Spiritual Aspects of Psychiatric Practice," formed the Oskar Pfister Award Lecture in San Francisco, May 26, 1993.

Dr. Fleischman practices psychiatry in Amherst, Massachusetts.

The Spiritual Aspects
of
Psychiatric Practice

THE SPIRIT OF HEALING
AND THE
BIO-PSYCHO-SOCIAL-SPIRITUAL
MODEL

There is a healing spirit (1). By "spirit" I mean a mood, an intangible yet definable ambiance that underlies and facilitates the restoration of well-being. In some circumstances, the healing spirit alone can reverse psychopathology, but more often it participates in complicated processes that include technical, psychological, and medical interventions which are buoyed up by it.

"Bedside manner" and "doctor-patient relationships" are quaint colloquial references to the healing spirit, which far exceeds in utility and complexity kindness and manners. It has been studied and practiced by every culture in every era of history, more or less consciously or thoroughly. At its fullest, the healing spirit guides a critical set of psychological attributes into vaulting life.

The healing spirit accompanies the work of the shaman, social worker, psychologist, family practitioner and surgeon. It also provides the leverage of the tele-evangelist, the cult guru, and the charismatic sectarian, because it rises from the deepest strata of the psyche, and ignites forces that, like humanity itself, can create or destroy.

Psychiatry as a discipline rooted in physical, biological, medical and social sciences, and in humanism, but focused primarily on the clinical contingency of illness and health, has had good vantage in studying and manifesting the healing spirit. Many of the Oskar Pfister Award winners honored by the American Psychiatric Association have been explicators and advocates for its beneficial atmosphere.

Jerome Frank, the first psychiatrist to receive the Oskar Pfister Award, wrote his classic, *Persuasion and Healing* (2), in answer to the question: what are the active ingredients of healing itself; what are its universal components? He pointed to a number of variables that I will discuss in a moment. Robert J. Lifton and Robert Coles, in their many books, extended elements of the healing spirit out towards social problems, global dilemmas, the human condition en masse, and have maintained the status of psychiatry as a profession for expansive minds and hearts. Viktor Frankl, who may well have written the most important one hundred or so pages of our century (3), is a spiritual Titan, who drew the gauze of love over the inferno and brought it back unsinged, then applied it to our mundane old wounds in individual psychotherapy.

Unfortunately, psychiatry has not adequately understood or utilized the healing spirit because of the cleavage between psychiatry and religion that Freud created with the hope of keeping his creation, psychoanalysis, free from what he felt to be the divisive and superstitious errors of religion. Oskar Pfister, the Swiss Protestant clergyman and Freud's loyal disciple and friend, tried to bridge the two professions. But the momentum set in motion by the great founder, who in the *Future of an Illusion* (4) referred to religion as a neurosis, remained unstoppable for most of our century. By ignoring or vilifying the great spiritual traditions rather than inquiring into them, psychiatry has lost access to helping knowledge and skills, and has fragmented its basic vision of human nature.

Organized religions, the major storehouse of spiritual energy, cannot be simply embraced by scientific and medical professions. Freud's awe and fear of them can't be casually discarded. The mystery of human nature, its abysmal evil and transcendent generosity, steams from the caldera of religion, that molten zone evoked to justify genocide, holy war, psalm and tea ceremony. An even greater mistake than ignoring the history and meaning of the human spirit as it is encoded in religion, would be to blindly adopt or apologize for it. As a secular profession, psychiatry needs to root itself in the study of religion as it does in the study of biology or psychology, not to refer to ourselves as Christian or Jewish or Buddhist psychiatrists, as a few of our colleagues are very mistakenly doing, any more than, because we are doctors, we would refer to ourselves as Kidney or Pineal psychiatrists.

The healing spirit *will* elude those who have an agenda to impose. Men and women who want to proclaim their private truths at the vulnerable and ill are not physicians. Doctors attend upon their patients, weighing advantage versus disadvantage with every sentence, careful to do no harm.

Study of the healing spirit has immediate value for the psychiatric clinician. It facilitates listening to, understanding, and empathizing with patients of diverse backgrounds, and helps the clinician reflect upon and control for his or her own beliefs and attitudes. It aids the scientific psychiatrist in affirming science and religion simultaneously, without being limited to reductionistic materialism, nor giving vent to personal, capricious, wish fulfillment. It affirms the continuity of individuals with social and historical forces. It alerts to dangers and opportunities. Study of the healing spirit leads to a receptive dialogue of inquiry, connecting through the suspended hum of warm words doctors, patients, texts, traditions, and flashes of light.

The healing spirit should not be hawked as an alternative to biological or other psychological treatments, but as a fulfillment, enrichment, or rounding off of other modalities, as a delivery vehicle in which they can be dissolved for maximum efficacy. Psychiatric maturation is always marked by a pacific attitude, in which layers of understanding flow at varying depths, in different directions, without eliminating their subducting opposites. I don't want to fragment, but to synthesize the great spheres of study upon which psychiatry stands. Today, let us launch the bio-psycho-social-spiritual model.

To understand the healing spirit, we have to dive deeply enough below the surface of religion, with its particular ideologies, rituals, and social affiliations, to discover a basic science of the spirit, that would expose its universal essence—of which particular religions are living manifestations. There we can locate a germinal bud, green with mitosis, where the same laws of life govern stem and heart, and springtime and hope are not metaphors for each other.

Psychiatry can address the human condition fully only when individual psychiatrists have wandered as disciples of the spirit, and have attained the competence to identify, befriend, and deliver it, when it appears sick before us in patients under our care.

To infuse this gnosis into our profession requires methods consonant with the goals.

SEVEN METHODS
OF MEETING
THE HEALING SPIRIT

The healing spirit is approached through an inclusive vision, a comprehensive viewpoint, based upon the question: How does the patient in front of me reflect or cause all the phenomena of humanity, its wisdom and wars and mass murders and guitar solos? This embracing perspective circumambulates the individual, listening for universal truths reverberating in discrete persons and moments. The healing spirit is revealed only when a whole person uses their own intuited entirety to relate to the patient's total darkness and potential. Without surrendering objectivity and self-scrutiny, the healing spirit is completed by intersubjectivity.

(2)

All religions are at least partly rooted in the isolated quest through dread in the labyrinth of the self. Therefore, the healing spirit is understood through loneliness and contemplation. By "contemplation," I am using a generic term for all disciplined, introspective concentration. Mere loneliness is a psychological desert, but it can be irrigated into fertility by all those modes of interiority that lead outside presuppositions, conventions, and existing paradigms. It is only during loneliness and contemplation that long strands of knowing can unravel and become dyed by sustained immersion in the spirit.

Both Freud and Jung endured lengthy wracking loneliness in exploration of their psychological depths. Yet isolation has limitations and dangers: Jung reminded us that his loneliest years, after his break with Freud, would have ended in insanity were it not for his family and his clinical responsibility, two essential guardians for a safe descent (5). Still, it is only the solo dreamer and explorer who brings back to the human community gems and geodes from the psychic underground.

(3)

The healing spirit is also approached via illuminated language, words that transmit the state they describe. Every spiritual knowing that lasts among people becomes embedded in poetic words: testaments, gospels, sutras and slokas. To follow the spirit, one must punctuate life with the pause given by reading these enduring, shimmering tablets through which the heart can recognize its own message and lineage.

Psychiatry and its allied professions have inherited the spiritual library of humankind, and have created their own wisdom texts that are as inspiring as they are empirical and informative, works by Freud, Jung, James, Fromm, and Oskar Pfister Award winners Viktor Frankl, Jerome Frank, Robert J. Lifton, Robert Coles, and many others. Master texts don't merely purvey information; they exude an aura. It is important to preserve as part of our professional formation and reeducation the seashore of language, beautiful and sonorous with the turbulent surf of the human spirit.

Without reverence for words, in whose symbolic galaxies the dust of our ideas cohere into comprehension, we stumble towards a dim future. Students who have memorized textbooks and formulas for a decade to become doctors, blind to the media in which their ideas dwell, will dispense prescriptions at twenty-minute intervals like a tribe of Skinner's white pets.

They will believe, rather than assess, the prose and charts of logical positivism in professional journals. This codified mono-culture of reflexive thought is far from the pondering that is necessitated by the com-plexity of the psychiatric task. To glimpse the healing spirit, psychiatrists require language that penetrates and saturates the fjords of experience.

(4)

The healing spirit flows between the riverbanks of culture. *Culture is the eager practice of elevating   relationships which encircle discipline, concentration, beauty, and emotional expression.*

Culture is the lumen through which spiritual nutrition flows to each cell, each individual. In a polytheistic multi-culture like our own, we contain Jewish culture, or African-American culture, or Italian Cath-olic culture, woven together into an almost illimitable and personalizable complexity. Still, we contact our own spirit only when the sweetened drops of collective human history pour into us. The bedrock of culture in general delimits where the channels of the spirit can flow within the interlocking matrices of human relations we call society, and directly impacts on individual pathology and recovery.

Two phenomena highlight the role that culture plays even in hard-core, neurobiological psychiatric syndromes: first, the more psychiatrists there are and the more money and energy spent on psychiatric research in a country, the worse the outcome of schizophrenia (6); second, after the decade of triumphal progress in diagnosing and treating depression, depression is more widespread. The more people we treat more effectively for depression, the more depression grows and, our leading epidemiologists assure us, this increase is not an artifact of either improved recognition or reporting (7).

There are many possible causes for each of these two phenomena, but together they challenge us to ask fundamental questions about our profession. At the very least, we have to challenge not only the validity of the data and of the interpretation of the data, but also the efficacy of case by case solutions to illnesses that may be as much cultural as individual. We have to ask: Is the totality of our professional activity ineffectual? Is the totality of our professional

activity harmful? No one has the answers to
these questions; the fissures that must be
spelunked to answer them extend far beyond
my topic. But when I remember some schizophrenic patients I saw in India—their
quiet days sitting on charpoys in the shade
of the earthen walls of their family home,
surrounded by the hubbub of joint familial
life yet tacitly excused from it, fed familiar
recipes by mothers and sisters without ex-
pectation of cure or change, receiving
occasional validation for their primary
process excursions into invisible, intangible
worlds (at least when those mental journeys
were not too bizarre or provocative)—I
don't feel mystified by the superior
prognosis of Indian schizophrenic patients
to American patients with the same syn-
drome, whose families insist they return to
Amherst College or Yale for a second try
and a second humiliating flunk-out, whose
social workers vie for power in the State
Department of Mental Health by documen-
ting how many of these patients they have
cajoled into living in rooming houses in
violent slums rather than with their
"regressive" families, and whose psychiatrists consider sialorrhea, obesity, and
exhaustion "no significant side effects," and
who consider disfiguring choreas and

zombified akinetics as vaguely acceptable costs for the attainment of lifelong exile into chaotic and anguished group apartments. If I become schizophrenic, mail me to Poona.

Autonomy is a worthy goal, but not the exclusively valuable human attainment. Some people, particularly schizophrenic patients with subtle deficits in cortical cellular organization or volume; or neural dysrhythmias; or deficits in information processing, startle or attention regulation; can only be coerced towards autonomy at the expense of their sanity. Treatment of the schizophrenias requires not only improvement in neurobiological interventions to modify underlying neurophysiological illness, but also appreciation for lifestyles that are of necessity rooted in passivity, daydreams, varying degrees of dependence, reverie, and speculation. The quiet and calming side of existence is a treasure to us all, but an essential niche for some. There is a very clear reason for the hundred-year-old psychiatric cliché that schizophrenics often show religious preoccupation. The schizophrenias are not only diseases: they are reminders which these people impose upon the rest of the human community, that fantasy and family caretaking are also threads in the loom of human life. A culture like our own, obsessed with independence and efficiency, will continue to find that injecting cures into schizophrenic patients will make them worse.

At the very moment our journals proclaim treatment resistant depression is now fully treatable, we find this illness, too, not eliminated, but commoner. Is it possible that depression is a product not only of individual events like our genes, our neurochemical predispositions, and our particular familial constellations, but also of *educational* backdrops like how many sonnets we can quote, and how many warblers we have welcomed as they migrated their masterful thousands of intercontinental tree-top miles in Spring? Didn't people once learn to study nature or to read old tomes in original languages not only for entertainment, but for the very purpose of buttressing the spirit through winter and bereavement and aging–into– death? Can depression spread worldwide as mass-media hypnosis supplants personal cultivation?

Humanness is a garden that needs tilling to flower. You can't diagnose "bad soil" merely because there are weeds in a neglected lot. Hundreds of millions of people on earth today grow up passive, electronic mass media appendages, who have never had the seeds of music or literature sown over them, nor been hoed by apprenticeship to kind, creative minds. How can anyone get through a New England winter or a New Dehli summer if they cannot hum to themselves lyrics to songs of fortitude and humor?

Would it be preposterous to you that, before we diagnose seasonal affective disorder, we have to rule out first starvation of the spirit, and that before we prescribe serotonin reuptake inhibitors or megalight, we first prescribe courses on Emerson and Thoreau and lessons in cross-country skiing—with its exposure to snow-sparkle? You cannot treat a human in isolation from their acquaintance with the historical foundation that enables us all to rise above hunter-gatherer scarcity.

I know many psychiatrists have met, as I have, some broken teenager locked incommunicado, until he or she plays out loud a cassette of what initially sounds like amplified convulsions, only for us to discover that, through the medium of music, the patient can now at least point to what he or she feels, and the doctor can hear melody and poetry in what initially sounded only like the dark side of the cerebellum.

I want to be clear that I do not consider schizophrenia and depression *merely* cultural. In my clinical practice, I live out validation for our profession's well-rounded emphasis on neurotransmitters, medications, family dynamics, cognitions, affects, dreams and internalized experiences. I am not involved with erasing or minimizing any therapeutic tools. I do not even daydream of a millenial era in which destructive syndromes like the schizophrenias and depression are *abolished* by social transformations. But the data we already have insists that we consider what percentage of these syndromes will continue to overpower our clinical skills and require wholesale social reorganization, as illiteracy requires schools.

According to William McNeil in his book, *The Rise of the West* (8), civilization is still being created and spread worldwide from its original seed. Civilization is still emerging and psychotherapy is part of that birth. Psychotherapy can be defined as *selective and sensitive integration of interpersonal modes of civilization with individuals uninformed or unable to have previously absorbed them.* As psychiatrists, we are not only modern doctors of clinical science that deals with serotonergic deficit syndromes and dopamine dysregulation, we are also ambassadors from Babylon, Jerusalem, Bodh-gaya, and Athens. Every psychiatric consulting room is a mission of dialogue, attention, satisfaction through relatedness, and appreciation of our common inheritance of thousands of years of wealth in knowledge of how to be cheerfully, productively and reasonably human.

The absence of culture is not a disease, and the misery it induces requires not treatment, but transfusion from the marrow of our common life. The healing spirit is also a vehicle of cultural education.

(5)

Professions can be learned, but they are resurrected and regenerated through the eminence of mentors and colleagues. We are prefigured by our best teachers, not by their knowledge but by their glow, which adumbrates a zone of safety and wonder to sanctuary the sick, and to provoke transgenerational renewal of the healing spirit. Psychiatry is partly learned, and partly conveyed. The amount of ourselves we can bring to bear in our clinical work is partly a function of the number of our pre-synaptic vesicles that our teachers, supervisors and colleagues induce into activity. Every one of those rare stimulators of open-endedness deserves the honorific title, "Synapse-Maker." As clinicians we can pass on to stuck minds that adaptation, that most salubrious game and joy, a mind without blind alleys, in which axons and dendrites arborize from each situation to infinity.

(6)

This conveyed aspect of the healing spirit, from culture to individual, from language to experience, from teacher to student, from doctor to patient (and, as I will soon discuss, from patient to doctor) is also a partly non-verbal, non-intellectual transmission that occurs through body language, ambient gestalt, through the vibration of presence. Our profession rightly concerns itself with the atmosphere of the ward, or the therapist's holding environment. The tenor and turgor of the healer's physical presence is one—albeit partial—component of the healing spirit. Our Harris tweeds, our

Oxford cloths and silks, communicate to patients. Not just words, but fields of self-projective emanations mingle as doctor and patient meet. Herein lies another small tool of the healing spirit.

(7)

Most importantly, as a method of approaching the healing spirit, the doctor listens to, observes, and absorbs the patient and their world. This vast arena, the bulk of our professional lives, I will try to discuss throughout the next main section.

TEN UNIVERSAL ELEMENTS
OF SPIRITUAL LIFE

Psychologically, all spiritual life encompasses ten repeating, universal themes. These function like elements, that are multivalent, and that recombine into complex emotional molecules to constitute either individual or organized spirituality. Whether spiritual life is solitary or communal, whether it is demonic or sanctifying, is a matter of which of these elements are combined and with what valences. The healing spirit is alive with the same psychic matter as witch burning, but the primeval plenipotential of this ground is given its particular direction by the spin on each of its elements and by the fullness of its cross-combinations.

The viewpoint I will take is synthesizing and multiplex. Stretching around polythematic mosaics, this viewpoint seeks to preserve complexity. It will not create a new school of thought, but hopefully will have a sparing effect against the pseudo-specialization of psychiatry into competing schools of biological or psychoanalytic reductionism.

The ten elemental themes of all spiritual life are observable in psychotherapies that explore personality deeply and widely. They are both data of therapy and, when understood, therapeutic.

I will depend upon the delineating, magnifying power of words to surround and explicate these numen of human heart and mind. To capture these force-fields in words requires more space than one paragraph; therefore, I can only be suggestive, rather than definitive. In the book, *The Healing Spirit*, where I first defined these ten universal themes, I bonded them to clinical examples; in this essay, the concepts are the same, but while cases cannot be included due to constraint of time, the linguistic seine I will throw around these energy nodes is entirely new prose for a new occasion.

ONE

Witnessed Significance

A human being is not complete unless he or she is known. The extent to which we are known will be a major subjective measure by which we will assess our life, our health, our well-being. Thus we confess and reveal ourselves to our lovers; thus someone will live in slums in order to paint the pictures their mind projects; thus someone will write over and against a stream of publishers' rejection letters or even government censors. This drive for witnessed significance is the hallmark of the psalms, and the promise of every anthropomorphic religion: that a divine eye is watching and a divine ear is listening to us. This is also the prow of every psychotherapeutic voyage: someone listens, someone understands. The wish to be identified and weighed in as valuable to others animates the human spirit. A historian who was trapped and starved in the Warsaw Ghetto left his first-hand account buried in bottles beneath the rubble, rats and corpses—we found his scribbled history book, and feel the triumph of his witness and its significance. Conversely, we listen to the story of the abrasive patient, who reveals to us how he never felt known or understood, and thereby we learn to empathize with this apparently selfish narcissist, whose drive for attention and importance becomes understandable.

Witnessed significance leads us forward to political activism, literary composition, and historical and even cosmic reflection, as well as to friendship and the mating of hearts that can accompany marriage. If it is not fulfilled constructively, however, this same element of the spirit will nevertheless be heard: the lonely borderline man shoots a prominent statesman, knowing that will at least get him onto worldwide television; the isolated teenager invents a psychotic universe of highly intrusive, deeply involved pseudo "others." The struggle to be heard, *truly*, with impact, is an intangible force in every person, a problem that contributes to psychiatric disorder, and an element of the healing spirit.

TWO

Lawful Order

A human being is driven to construe order in and around him or herself. We see the urge to understand and recreate a lawful universe in the religious mind, which speaks to us of a guiding, structuring presence orchestrating the whole. The same need for lawful order also prompts the scientific quest to reduce events to patterns.

Within individual lives there is a need to understand oneself that may be profound and curious, or superficial and authority-based, but it is never absent. A person deprived of self-understanding will search for it. There is nothing more common to psychotherapeutic clinicians from every discipline and from every school of thought than the gift of explanation. The human animal must pattern perceptions into a lawful order and must fit him or herself into that embracing description; and this drive unites the external cosmos with *personal* continuity, self-knowledge, and identity.

If we keep in mind the words "lawful order," we can snap together into one frame an array of phenomena: the pathologies of frenetic counter-order, like anorexia; the religious fanatic who must construe the world in a certain way and would rather die (and sometimes does) than shift point of view; or the lifelong curiosity that marks the most creative and productive minds. Lawful order is the source of authoritarianism and orthodoxy, with their salves of absolute certainty; and is one drive building the fortress mentality of obsessionals. Lawful order is a felt pressure in people, expanding into diverse forms, depending on its personal developmental vicissitudes.

Scratch a person, and you'll get their explanations. Offer good explanations, and you will find followers. Explore interior problems, puzzlements, and solutions, gently probing to find troubling perplexity, then stimulating solutions that can endure empirical trials, and you are a psychotherapist, not only helping, but harnessing a timeless spiritual element into a healing process.

The fruition of lawful order ripens among those who feel themselves held aloft on the palm of a comprehensible, predictable, fundamentally trustworthy world, and who can spread that confidence, security, and competence to others.

THREE

Wholeness

To bring us to fullness, the emotional, spiritual forces within us drive the multiplex mammal we are towards wholeness. The gustatory, fornicating animal, the herd-hider and crowd-chanter, the philosopher, poet, hobo—each of those are in each one of us, and must be woven into an organized man or woman. Wholeness requires an affirmation of our totality, the ability to uplift, incorporate, and synthesize, rather than to repress, split off, or deny. At our best we bring to bear on the problems of each day our instinctual, cerebral, and ethical attributes in mutually abeyant, focal heat.

But along with affirmation, we have to learn acceptance of our limits, disabilities, and conflicts. Acceptance is the maturational, modulating antithesis to affirmation. To be whole, we have to accept that we cannot fully affirm and can never be whole. We are set to expand into and synthesize all we are, yet we are never smoothly homogeneous, always time-limited, space-limited, shadowy and unsanded.

Therefore, wholeness is a mixture of affirming-acceptance in a whirling dynamic. When it malfunctions, affirming-acceptance can produce overweening self-affirmation: the hypomanic, narcissistic, entitled psychopathologies erupt from this. The opposite malfunction also occurs: no self-affirmation, dependence, anxiety, withdrawal, avoidance of living.

Wholeness is seasoned, ironically, through *detachment*, that Indian summer of emotional life, from which vantage the hills and valleys of one's days are all seen in one fond, fading landscape.

Religions have always and will continue to tinker with this spiritual teeter-totter; you will hear them talking about it according to their theologies of original sin, absolution, confession, Yom Kippur or Ramadan: ideas, rituals, occasions that surround the tension of becoming whole, all you are; yet also relinquishing, giving-over-to, bowing.

To heal hurt humans, psychiatrists need to know how to tune the forces of the spirit so that the whole person is drawn forth, every potential note sung, yet cacophonies reduced, and cadences struck to control otherwise directionless flow. There is no "correct" or final note for affirming-acceptance. Tension on strings makes music.

FOUR

Calling

At one interval of their lives, every young human animal will awaken and seek a particular obligation, responsibility, task to be imposed upon them by the conjunction of their existence with the vaults of history. Every person yearns for a calling. Today, most are defeated and broken, slinking back into prudence, convention, and prescription.

Every religion addresses this element of the spirit, more or less effectively. Some religions provide group callings: Our caste is born to serve in this manner—join us; or We are the priests to humankind. Others necessitate a vision quest, in which each young man (but not woman) gains a unique name and role. Others foster individuation through solitary prayer. The Protestant reformation, with its origin in the journey to individual vocation through unmediated personal relationship to God, and with its lava flow of economic license, anti-authoritarian participatory rule, fusion of prosperity with blessedness, individualistic guilt and anxiety, and material mastery, quite possibly is the most forceful spiritual eruption ever to flow from humanity. Will it end in widespread freedom of conscience, or ecological excoriation and death of planet earth?

Activate the sense of calling, and you create a meteor, for better or worse. Called heroes die for their cause. Called villains commit suicide in service of theirs. Called artists and scientists endure isolation to pursue the answer and the beauty they know is theirs alone to find. Called psychotics torture children in the name of their sanctifying cult.

The emergence of a calling feels so fated, inevitable, yet mysterious that it rekindles descriptions of "rebirth," as if an individual comes to be *in order* to fulfill the calling. Even so, calling is never a product of narcissistic self-appointment, for, in Erickson's re-statement of the wisdom of gurus, one must be identified in order to gain identity (9). A therapist may sometimes provide the interiorizing attention and self-reorganization that enables calling to be heard.

A calling is heard from within, when the spiral of identity biopsies eternity. No doctor knows their patient's calling, but the good psychotherapist sits back and deciphers, within the contractures of the patient's complaints, echoes of great necessities, and reflects them back. Sometimes they accrete mass and momentum and a new spirit emerges from the healing. But a rigid and callow society can crush the forming sphere, permitting no room for flight. You can't launch a chariot to heaven in an astrodome. The ball field of the spirit has no roof.

FIVE

Membership

As social mammals, we are born to run with the pack. Anyone who was ever thirteen remembers the poignant, urgent desperation with which membership is studied and sought. A calling can be heard anywhere, anytime, but it flashes into life only within relationships. Some people belong to their nation or their era; others' belonging is limited to their family; those who belong nowhere invent or hallucinate their group. "The touch of the crowd" as Elias Canetti called it (10), is a biological drive; its internal representation is transmuted by human feeling, intuition and spirit into an essential pneuma, membership. Soldiers, fraternity boys, gang members will die just to feel it tumble reassuringly around their shoulders for a moment before they go. Religions will manipulate it with their "elect," their "chosen people," their "Brahmins," and their "saved." Parareligious nation-states mobilize mass suicide-murder by promising membership.

Membership can suffocate other spiritual elements, like wholeness, or it can drain the energy of other elements like witnessed significance, so that the atom feels seen and known as part of the glorious horde in which it surges. Houdinis of the spirit twist free of membership for a breathless moment to find their unique wholeness or calling, but they must at last return to it if they are to avoid the aridity and bitterness of ostracism or isolation.

Membership is the media of human participation, interpenetration with other lives, people, animals, plants, historical forces like scientific "progress" or "freedom," a church, a people, felt connections to the supervening, non-material, unseen. Through membership, the mineral and invisible cosmos . . . gains a face. The child twinkles with giddy excitement among his friends. The grandmother dies confidently if daughters and grandsons surround and shield her from the vacuum of the universe's swallowing opacity. Not every invisible friend is a fantasy.

Psychotherapists provide idealized memberships of one, that they hope will generalize. They teach balance of availability and privacy, attention and limits, care and termination. They catalyze fawning and

snarling group predators into familial, political, choral people. Carefully refraining
from the false affectation of friendship,
they reveal that the impersonal universe
converges unexpected goodness into bifoc-
aled, besuited professionals who dispense
both Blue Cross forms and receptive, mutual
humanity.

SIX

Release

To a greater or lesser extent for each
individual, mundane life is unbearable. To
say this is to break a pervasive taboo. As
psychiatrists we may hear in any one week
half a dozen people tell us they are sui-
cidal; even as we are aware that on any one
day millions of people court death via
alcohol, tobacco, drugs; and almost every-
one submits to mental coma by television.
Still, though we find our own lives filled
with warmth and curiosity that we hope will
last until our nineties, we can't block out
the wisdom of our spirit reflected in the
depths of every religious tradition: death is
inevitable, loss is inevitable, decay and
disease are inevitable, life is inextricably
woven with suffering. Every child who
leaves the sunshine of hopes, and enters
adult actualities, nurtures a damaged heart.
No matter how fortunate, every man and
woman covets release.

Religions promise release in the next

life, or in their soothing ritual. Atheistic cynicism delivers release via the down-regulation of hope and care into gray resignation. Excitements of youth seek to blast away awareness of mortality, war, injustice, the horrible and mountainous unacceptability of earthly conditions, at the very moment these succubae peak in consciousness—when the secure circle of parental safety is abandoned, and the glare of the human condition is encountered head-on. We seek a god, a heaven, a nirvana, a drug, a drunkenness, a sexual mode, a future fantasy of scientific or political progress, a personal fame or wealth, because the holocausts, the schiz-ophrenias, the incests, the political tor-tures, our own fears and defeats drive us toward release. We dream of surcease, and rebirth, because the factual crust of the world does not feed our spirit.

Release at its worst fuels pathetic fan-tasy escapes; at its best, it is a matura-tional function that combines integration with one's own body; confidence in human society; and faith in the unraveling and pregnant future. Here each individual honors, through internalization, the poet, folk singer, paradigm-forging scientist, clergy, or visionary, who swaddles us in what we still can hope is possible. When you release control, what subtends you? Release requires a sense of lawful order in the world, a worthy membership, a meaningful task well done, and personal wholeness.

The psychiatrist uses his or her own depth and complexity of release to help patients who cannot rest, relax, accept, let go, sleep. Much of our professional day is spent medicating, educating, and ministering to people in whom these release functions are undeveloped or broken. Freud, our high priest, taught patients and doctors to *dream*, because, unlike animals who merely slumber, in unconsciousness we humans continue to suffer and envision. Even the release of sleep requires competent dreaming.

Release may begin as basic trust in our mothers' arms, but it can't remain that simple; we learn to be held by friends and faiths as transition to not being held at all. All children at some stage fear darkness and sleep. How do we learn to relinquish daylight and our*selves*?

Oskar Pfister Award winner Hans Küng has written that God is by nature ahead of us, before us. For Küng, God is not about *accepting* the world, but about the exfoliation of the new, the good, from within the disappointing actuality already past. I would like to amend Küng's inspired words, to say that for *all healing* orientations, the present "now" is not definitive; but "future" is mere fantasy; between now and the next moment is a momentum of reality beyond factuality. With or without the word "God," a man or woman entrained to hopeful spirit, releases the husk of sorrow, and with faith reshapes the world.

Release results from a felt intuition, that there is a validation for why we *all* inwardly feel so promised. The healing spirit that fulfills life also reveals that death is a doorway.

SEVEN

World View

The phrase that God created humans in his image means that every person is also the creator. Each individual lives in a totality they create from their own experiences, education, culture, fantasy, aspirations and defeats. This psychic cosmos, or world view, may be conscious, extensive, complex with coves and islands like the Maine coast, or it may be simple, reflexive and dimly lit. When we make the effort to really encounter a person, we walk into another *world*, with its theology, laws, morality, history, populace, gods, demons, and heroes. Possibly the greatest gift that Freud and psychiatry in general have given to the human condition, is the belief that an extensive journey by a doctor into the Aegean of an unknown, undistinguished person's psyche, is valuable. Due to the Freudian revolution, it is an accepted position in American society that the inner wrinkles, memories, and shades of feeling in anyone's life are worthy of exhumation and expression. Hundreds of thousands of worlds have come alive, sprung free, through psychotherapy.

The attentive and evoking healer raises from the shadow world of unexpressed secrecy the creative stylus of world views, that are transformed by the very act of being illuminated. Millions of people today seek psychotherapy and expect to tell and to be heard. Psychotherapists in their chairs are always rafting down some unexplored Amazon.

But private world views can not only be suffocating prisons, they can also be expropriating parasites that seek to drain or smother every abutting dreamer. Psychotherapy without careful attention to diagnosis, prognosis, ego strengths and character has unleashed destructive organisms infecting their surroundings with strident complaining, self-expression at the expense of listening, and the terrible delusion that self-fulfillment means permission to lacerate anyone who stands in the way.

The over-eager application of psychotherapy has unleashed wild worlds that have spun free of the meridians. Restraint and reverence are the longitude and latitude of the heart.

Every world view has an omphalos that connects it to a cosmic other, bigger, outer. Proper psychotherapeutic intervention includes intimations of respect and gratitude, without which world views dry into meteors that bash about in entitled distress until they fragment into dust—allergenic for the neighbors. Well intended but unbalanced, monotonic overemphasis on empathy may inadvertently inculcate self-preoccupation, and block the equally important psychotherapeutic purveying of externally framed alternative viewpoints. Doubt is the rudder of adaptation.

Every sane world view takes into account its own incompleteness and knows that the stars are pinholes emitting light from a beyond. Didn't Socrates create Western philosophy with the insight that wisdom is always framed with a question mark?

EIGHT

Love

When I hear stories of couples traveling together towards death across the ocean of life, or of parental devotion in ministering to impaired children, or of poets enduring in wonder against the ticking of routine, I feel a majesty within humanity, as if the drummer boy and the flower girl, soon to be restored as prince and princess, are still wandering incognito yet radiant among us. The king and queen have been discovered. It is love that coronates men and women and elevates them for our fealty. By love I do not mean merely the sexual and the amorous, but human love, the capacity to feel unbounded outflowing care and affection—confiding and revered mutuality.

Love ultimately wafts across all barriers, even death. Every one of us has felt the love of some inspired naturalist, writer, or saint reach out across a hundred or a thousand years and pull us against the bosom of an ideal we will hold for the rest of our lives. At its strongest, love is indeed the panacea, the unstormable refuge; and in its commoner, less august form, it eases our individuality into marriage or parenting or service to orphans and old trees. Human love is how we transcend our frame, to flock and soar among timeless aspirations. It carries us past castration fears and private time, into the timeless flow of generosity and help, by which soil gives nutrient to pine, or educators pass on literacy, ethics, and avocations.

The talking cure was also called the cure by love (11). Of course, it would have been arrogant for psychiatry to have dubbed itself the medical specialty with expertise in love. No one can claim an expertise so subtle and lofty. Unfortunately, our profession has tumbled to the opposite extreme.

In a typical residency training program in psychiatry, love is not on the curriculum. The ultimate measure of competence in psychiatry currently consists of memorizing answers to a multiple choice exam and demonstrating cunning in a half-hour interview. We have defined ourselves in this affectless manner with our training and our certifications. Like our depressed patients, we have created a persona to induce a demeaning response from those who have very accurately understood how we view ourselves.

Human beings can love, can suffer from the failure to love, and can revive with love as their beckoning light. Someone will heal the spirit with love, but if psychiatrists are only created and assessed by their ability to reproduce right answers in certification rituals, this great treasure of healing will pass out of our professional realm to be practiced by others with no professional training or restraints at all.

Patients who can understand and afford it will continue to purchase psychotherapy that incorporates the life of their spirit. But duped citizens, who are told they are purchasing mental health care, only to have a few sessions parceled out in begrudging alliquots, are being cheated, not because their medications will be less effective, but because they do not come under the care of a healer who catalyzes their humanity. These patients will be fixed by strategists repairing broken machines.

Those who practice the cure by love do not dispense it. Therapists who love their patients ensnare them in a trap. Doctor and patient attend upon the release of this natural function from under the defeat and hatred that buried it. The doctor cleans the wound; new tissue must multiply itself on the new site. Doctors love with the restraint of New England climate, that dispenses short, lush summers among long arctic winters, a regimen that culminates in the victory of fibrous old oaks. At its rare best, psychotherapy enables the growth of a love that shatters the treatment and grows resilient and shade-giving far beyond the scope of the broken nut who once cupped it in husk and solicitude.

NINE

Sacrifice

Why don't we fill more journal pages, more conferences, more insurance-reimbursement-liaison committees with discussions of how draining it is to be a psychiatrist? It's exhausting! The keenness of continuous psychotherapeutic attention to others is a honing that, like sharpening a knife edge, continuously rubs away shards of self. But few would relinquish this profession of uniquely confidential and intimate privilege, because the sacrifice is worth it. In all ennobling acts there is sacrifice. We differentiate the spiritual from the mundane by the degree of emphasis on sacrifice of personal whim in favor of exalted service.

In recent years, sacrifice has been glassed under as a museum piece by a society that emphasizes self-expression, self-enhancement, and self-fulfillment. This contempt and rejection of sacrifice has a kernel of wisdom, for no virtue is more subject to abuse. Soldiers slaughtered for a tyrant's ambition, women under lifelong house-arrest in rigid gender roles, peasants brow-beaten by authoritarian religions, are all herded into their corner with the cattle-prod, "sacrifice."

Yet no liberation from the confines of narcissistic preoccupation can occur without the psychological ability to doff, to donate, to sacrifice. Contemporary life and psychotherapy must continue to search for authentic, relevant modes of being that steer between imprisonment within oneself and self-abnegation that mutilates. True sacrifice has always been rheostatic, constantly readjusting the current to avoid both selfishness and mortification. Sometimes, merely daring to enter and pursue psychotherapy is a heroic sacrifice for the confidentially anonymous citizen who must face his or her own perversions, addictions, and inadequacies head-on. There are still ways and occasions for the halo of sacrifice to overspread the edges of our trivial preoccupations and to buff them into occasions for hand-to-hand sacrifice in our common struggle for humane community. We can wisely remain chary of the exotic, upstaging "sacrifice" of self-serving grandeur.

Psychotherapy serves many patients who

need freedom from crippling guilts induced by someone else's demand that they sacrifice (of course, any sacrifice in compliance to someone else's demand isn't sacrifice at all, just subservience). Unfortunately, psychotherapy has too often ignored the opposite pole; the necessity of self-diminishing service and solicitude as an essential vitamin in spiritual nutrition, and so psychiatry shares responsibility for the cycle of anguish that the intrinsically faulty search for more has brought upon us.

The practice of psychotherapy alone is not a spiritual act, but it serves as an example that within the best of the secular glow nuggets of the spiritual. Every person desires to be able to sacrifice, for in that mental state a shutter opens and transcendence of self, if only momentarily, can be glimpsed shining like a sun.

TEN

Meaningful Death

If you raise a child you will steer a neophyte repeatedly through the corridor of death-awareness. Just as it seems incomprehensible to us now that our ancestors of one hundred years ago could have denied that robust, giggling, gawking and questioning childhood sexuality that Freud unveiled and that now seems so pervasive and obvious, so the role of death in the formation of character has attracted enough research and writing that it can no longer be closeted (12). The child sees his grandfather die, stomps on ants, listens to storybooks of heroes long-dead, and creates a sense of his or her own life in reference to hundreds of images and experiences of loss, destruction, cessation, death. The awareness of death molds character, starting with toddler-hood.

The navigator in each human existence glances through the sextant and perceives the horizon. We live in the paradoxical momentum of the finite crossing the immobility of the infinite.

Our "unconscious" includes not only repressed personal memories, but also those dimly apprehended, shattering pulses of the external whole, as they surge in and out of the meanings and proportions with which we gate and measure our life.

Religion and culture should facilitate passage through death's repeatedly encountered archway. But the enormous disjunction between the old religious myths with their concrete, household dimensions, and their paranoid-narcissistic landlords, measured against scientific imagery of dinosaur eras and black hole spaces, has left us naked, individual, and predominantly denying. A common response of many people to awareness of their own death is an agitated denial via group narcissistic inflation: if only we can lord it over someone else, we can feel immortal. We create what Erickson called "pseudo-species" (13) to distract ourselves into rage and power with the ensuing fight.

The ability to construct a meaningful death originates in childhood, is built on experience and overt and covert education and thought, and expresses itself in our values, actions, and our lived religion.

Meaningful death is not an issue limited to the terminally ill. It is a lifelong theme, that animates or constricts living, located in the cognitions of depressed patients, in the assumptions connected to panic, in adolescent turmoil, and in sexual compulsions. But today churchgoer and cynic alike share deep atheism, an absence of conviction that they will ever feel the universal ocean flowing in the estuary of their own blood.

Meaningful death is a migration, an untranslatable message that stirs flight in indefinable direction with unstoppable conviction, like autumn geese. Religion is not what you attest, but what you feel beneath you in the wind.

As doctors we can attempt to unclip our patients' wings of *quest*, which is the spiritual motion that enables our species to feel connected to time and space beyond personal death. Every human being possesses an organ, whose function is to receive messages about the direction of transcendent good.

THREATS TO THE
HEALING SPIRIT
IN PSYCHIATRY

Psychiatry is always in danger of being reduced to a para-profession whose practitioners follow fixed manuals and perform technical procedures on psychological or physiological systems. This danger was present even before psychiatry matured into its current form, and lies embedded in the matrix from which psychiatry was mined—as democracies rise from primitive organizations of government and must hold themselves aloft against the undertows of chauvinism and authoritarianism.

Our profession correctly prides itself on its roots in the work of Pinel, Kraepelin and Freud. Our founders were preceded by penal systems, dungeons, whippings and ostracism. Psychiatry arose in the tension between expression and repression, liberty and imprisonment, sympathy and sadism. Moment by moment, psychiatry takes shape from vast social forces, including but not limited to its own voices that sculpt empathic concern and empirical efforts against the rejection of illness and the desire for power that psychiatric disorders, with their

pain and frailty, induce. It was only fifty
years ago that Germany began its programs
of mass murder by testing the world community for its response to psychiatric euth-
anasia, and found there was little objection.

Psychiatry is intrinsically in tension
with forces that fear freedom of the spirit.
Free speech, even between doctor and
patient in confidential privacy, is always an
opening, and a threat to those (including at
times both doctor and patient) who feel ben-
efit from repression, secrecy and silence.
The resistance to psychiatry that may at
times wear an economic or technical mask,
is a recurrent reaction to the essence of the
profession.

Repressive forces reside in social in-
stitutions. Psychiatry has been one partici-
pant among many in opening airwaves and
hearts to the voices of victims of sexual
abuse, holocaust survivors, women corralled
by patriarchy, men broken by militarism,
and families dissolved by the subsidized
culture of alcoholism. Following closely
upon this upsurge in the quest for witnessed
significance, wholeness, membership, and
release by previously inchoate groups, a
new social movement arises to inform America that while mental illness is now re-
cognized and medications can help, talking

therapy is too expensive and must be cut short.

All forms of free expression are expensive. We could avoid unnecessary duplication of services if we had only one newspaper in the nation. If only one man governed, we could avoid the inefficient debates and added costs of Congress, courts and state government. In fact, the shaded, textured variations in people, in conversations, and over time, are the essence of respect for individuality that is the common basis of both healing and democracy.

As the middle class has discovered and will proceed with regardless of what happens to insurance benefits of groups more easily fooled or pushed, psychotherapy is an investment. To the college student who has dropped out in dismay, thousands of dollars invested in psychotherapy may produce half a million dollars in improved lifetime earnings when he or she returns to higher education, motivated for a self-selected career that feels called. For a couple who avoid divorce after investing tens of thousands of dollars in both individual and couples therapy, the money saved merely by avoiding rent or mortgage on two domiciles over a lifetime, amounts to hundreds of thousands of dollars. The depressed diabetic adolescent, who neglects or abuses insulin, may be spared maiming and early death, and tens of thousands of dollars in hospital bills, by an effective family psychotherapy that facilitates mature and reliable adjustment to a life on medication, and that enables parents to accept that their child cannot fulfill their own image of what he or she was supposed to have been. And for the major illnesses we treat—depression and the schizophrenias—we are indebted to senior biological psychiatric researchers like David Kupfer who are producing quantitative data to document that limited treatment may, in the long run, be very costly when compared to thorough and vigorous treatment that lessens recurrence.

Long term psychotherapy that releases the caged spirit to stretch and arise, contributes to the hubbub of freedom that offends groups who had benefited from the antecedent silence. Psychotherapy saves human and financial resources in the long run, but there is a wing of society that yearns to crush it and finds short term cost to be a convenient excuse.

Repressive forces also reside in patients. This of course was Freud's great discovery and need not be elaborated here, for throughout the civilized world his insight has been incorporated: we all to a greater or lesser extent fear our memories. Our days as psychiatrists are spent helping people remember what they felt, speak what they feel, face what they know. Our patients themselves, out of dread, may seek to abort the healing spirit. The psychiatrist balances timing, level of pain, and spoken truth in the pans of clinical skill. Free speech is a continuum. Those of us who sit in chairs all day for our profession often lift and sweat as much as the town road crew outside our office doors.

Repressive forces also reside in the doctor. Every properly trained psychiatrist observes within him or herself the ascendancy or exhaustion of interest in the patient dozens of times within one hour. This play of porousness and defense within the doctor serves him or her as a professionally honed dial of relatedness. But many psychiatrists we know are relieved to believe in impersonal mechanisms and low temperatures.

Ultimately, our treatment of others is based upon the way we follow our own spirit. Doctors will not adopt healing modalities of dogma and expediency if they construe their self-knowledge from a concatenation of cultural background, historical moment, temperamental style, biological strengths and deficits, parenting received and withheld, formative experiences, self cultivation, friendships, visions, dreams, choices, gifts, grace, and grit.

UNIFYING
PSYCHIATRY

Every sentence we speak in clinic, consulting room and hospital rounds molds our profession. We are constantly defining our work *by* our work. Against the resistances that would drive the healing spirit out of psychiatry, we can levy preeminently our daily lives. Excellence is always a form of defiance. Our greatest weapon in preserving the whole, multi-facetted profession of psychiatry is perseverance in speaking what we know under all circumstances in quiet sentences. Teachers and actors tell us that quiet sentences are heard better than yelled ones, since the listeners must suddenly lean forward and actively strain to hear.

Throughout, I have touched on five continuous applications that will keep the healing *spirit* alive among our equally important but often overweening healing *tactics*.

(1)

End rhetorical division within the profession. All psychiatrists can aver that little is known; there are many approaches; let us embrace our round profession. As a psychiatrist with a psychological and spiritual tint, I want to express my gratitude to my colleagues who have designed, studied, or delineated medications I have prescribed, for whose help I have then been praised and thanked by patients, from which I received the glow of feeling I had helped someone, when behind me stood the legions of bioneuropharmacological researchers. The *American Journal of Psychiatry*, the *Archives of General Psychiatry*, the *Journal of Clinical Psychiatry*, and *Biological Therapies in Psychiatry Newsletter* provide me the information I need to dispense medications that reduce extremes of mental anguish, as is sometimes necessary to enable conversations that can contain the healing spirit.

(2)

Our journals must expand to reflect our profession, not just our technology—most particularly, the *American Journal of Psychiatry*, which is supposed to be the organ of the American Psychiatric Association. Just as the Oskar Pfister Award keeps alive a critical aspect of psychiatry at the annual meeting, the *American Journal* ought to reflect in some part of every issue the human story. We can demand and reinforce this with our letters, our articles, our subscriptions and votes. Look at the *Journal of the American Medical Association*, spangled with art, poetry and personal narrative among its austere technicality. Our journals are obsessively overfocused on one elixir: the prosaic. Prosaic is S.S.R.I., which stands for stultifying spiritual religious ignorance.

(3)

The students we select, the ways we educate and inspire, and the manner by which we certify have all been mentioned here. Our profession is people, and the way they are grown defines our span. I hope no future psychiatrists will ever merit the dubious distinction bestowed upon some of the doctors of New Jersey in my childhood: "He's not a doctor—he's a specialist'"

(4)

In psychiatry to a unique degree this general principle is true: The healer is the healing. I became a psychiatrist because it was the only profession I heard of in which I could read almost anything, meditate on nothing, and travel almost anywhere, and still feel I was growing professionally. Psychiatry is the outflow of the imaginative identification of psychiatrists with suffering. Deepening ourselves is a professional pleasure and duty, for our profession will be as wide as our own lives.

(5)

Act as an organized professional membership to define ourselves and not be passively dictated to. Women's liberation, gay liberation, African-American politics have reminded us of the power of outspoken common identity. Do our patients know that psychiatrists pay approximately $4,000 x 30,000 members = $120,000,000 per year in malpractice insurance, every penny of which comes from patients' pockets? Why doesn't a card in every psychiatrist's office simply relate this one fact? How would that impact on malpractice reform legislation? Frightened, guarded, beleaguered professionals cannot work with a healing spirit.

AT
THE CONFLUENCE
OF RIVERS

To be able to continuously select the healing spirit in the face of repression, exhaustion, and unknowing, the psychiatrist must set up as a lifelong work habit a screen of receptivity capable of configuring it. The schema I have outlined here, with seven methods of exploring the healing spirit and ten elemental themes within it, is after all more poetics than physics. Just as the most sacred ground is often located at the confluence of two rivers, everything I have tried to say has only two components: care and discovery. The tides of ideas change, but these twins, like wind and water, will carry long, long life.

For discovery, the awake healer will divine individual variability in every function in each person. The world is fluid. For care, the healing spirit conjoins precise particularizing of people and their problems to *pragmatic* compassion: help, help first, before purity of doctrine or school. The healing spirit should not be construed as something always soft and soothing; sometimes it harnesses the force of feared sentences and firm reins. Worldly hands are required to belay lives that are in danger of slipping off the rock face of life.

The perspective of the healing spirit cannot be invoked by any reductionism without dissipating. Its tendrils entwine and incorporate other branches of psychiatric knowing. If the spirit of healing is maintained in robust health, it will prevent the pseudospecialization of psychiatry into schools competing with each other—like children playing king of the mountain—for temporary status as exclusive and complete truths about human nature. Science and religion have both observed the history of ideas rising and passing like a tide.

The backdrop perspective of the healing spirit implies time, a long time that holds many truths. In whatever we do to help, there could be another answer, another wrinkle, another firm refusal, another trial. The facts of healing are professionally informed actions, but the healing spirit has an exit door opening up to a milky way glittering with questions. Scientific, not technical education is the best training for a practitioner of the healing spirit, because science is the religion of never being satisfied with answers and never ceasing to hunt for new ones.

In summary, the healing spirit is that attitude which understands that, along with causal forces that do indeed shape us, there are the *spirits* with which we align ourselves. Though we are never free of psychological, biological, and social cause, we can choose within our cavern to follow urges and inklings that flutter and phosphoresce before us in half-light flight until, in a moment, our mind bursts forth into the blooming, acalendric Spring that we call spiritual life.

A psychiatry that aims to alleviate biopsychosocial distress but does not take into account this spiritual journey and plunge, is less efficient, less humane, and is itself a force of human diminution. Our synapses connect not only across to memory and emotion, but up and down to Hades and Olympus. Many human lives have been saved by the right metaphor.

Freud had a grand vision that psychiatry supplant religions with the common core of all religious good: "The alleviation of suffering and the brotherhood of man" (14). If this is too masculine or too naive for us today, I hope our profession will continue to at least emulate the scope of his calling. Psychiatry as a profession is inspirational because it retains practical goals, at the same time that it suffuses out toward the edges of the knowable. Properly practiced, psychiatry always has as its focal point nothing less than the re-elevation to freedom of thought, feeling, relationship, and spirit.

NOTES

(1) Fleischman, Paul. *The Healing Spirit: Explorations in Religion and Psychotherapy*. New York: Paragon House, paperback ed., 1990. The book elaborates Section III of this essay, providing full discussion, references, and clinical cases. It is available from Paragon House Publishers, 90 Fifth Avenue, New York, NY, 10011.

(2) Frank, Jerome. *Persuasion and Healing, A Comparative Study of Psychotherapy*. New York: Schocken Books, revised edition, 1974.

(3) Frankl, Viktor. *Man's Search for Meaning*. New York: Washington Square Press, 1963.

(4) Freud, Sigmund. *The Future of an Illusion*. Found in the Standard Edition of the *Complete Psychological Works*

of Sigmund Freud. London: Hogarth Press, 1953/1974.

(5)   Jung Carl. *Memories, Dreams, Reflections.* Edited by A. Jaffé. New York: Random House, 1961.

(6)   These findings were originally reported in: WHO (1973), *Report of the International Pilot Study of Schizophrenia*: Vol. I, Geneva, and WHO (1975), *Schizophrenia: A Multi-National Study*, Public Health Papers, No. 63, Geneva. The results were confirmed subsequently in: Sartorius, et. al., "Two-year follow-up of the patients included in the WHO International Pilot Study of Schizophrenia," *Psychological Medicine*, 1977, no. 7, pp. 529-541.
While results of one study are far from conclusive, even more so since the study antedated increasingly reliable diagnostic nomenclature and procedures; nevertheless, there are two salient outcomes from these WHO findings.
(1) The findings have never been

refuted. In other words, while these studies cannot be said to have proven that schizophrenia has a better prognosis in less developed countries, these findings do demonstrate that psychiatric research and treatment in developed countries do not yet have any proven positive outcome, and can reasonably be suspected of having a negative overall impact.

(2) The staggering implications of the WHO reports have been suppressed from our professional literature, which ought to be rife with dialogue and attempts to disprove the WHO findings. Kaplan, H.I. and Sadock, B.J., *Synopsis of Psychiatry*, 6th ed., Williams & Williams, 1991, p. 324, states succinctly, "Schizophrenia is prognostically more benign in less developed nations where patients are reintegrated into their families and communities more completely than they are in more highly civilized (sic) Western societies."

(7)   Cross and The National Collaborative Group, "The Changing Rate of Major Depression," *Journal of the*

American Medical Association, Dec. 2, 1992, vol. 268, no. 21.

(8) McNeil, William. *The Rise of the West*. Chicago: University of Chicago Press, 1963.

(9) Erickson, Erik. *Insight and Responsibility*. New York: Norton, 1964, pp. 90 and 125.

(10) Canetti, Elias. *Crowds and Power*. New York: Continuum Publishing, 1962.

(11) "Freud wrote in a letter to Jung in 1906, 'Psychoanalysis is in essence a cure through love.'" Quoted from Bettleheim, Bruno. "Freud and the Soul," *New Yorker*, March 1, 1982, p. 52.

(12) See, for example, Lifton, Robert J. *The Broken Connection*. New York: Simon & Schuster, 1979, Chap. 5.

(13) Erickson, Erik. *Gandhi's Truth*. New York: Norton, 1969. Special reference to pp. 194-195.

(14)   Freud, Sigmund. *Future of an Illu-
        sion*, op. cit.

OSKAR PFISTER AND SIGMUND FREUD: FRIENDSHIP WITHOUT A CLOUD

Oskar Pfister was born in Switzerland in 1873, the year that Sigmund Freud entered medical school; and, following his father's profession, he became a pastor in Zurich. In 1908 he discovered Freud's writing and his "old premonitions became reality" [(2) p. 190]. He wrote an essay, "Fantasy and Schoolboy Suicide," which his friend and fellow pastor's son, Carl Jung, recommended he send to Freud. This opened a literary, professional, and personal friendship that would last three decades, spanning nationalities and religions in an era of violence and vitriol, and that sailed through Freud's cantankerousness, ending only with Freud's death.

Pfister is described as tall, vigorous, handsome, warm and quiet, sporting bushy mustachios and black clerical robes. Freud, his children, and his biographers speak of Pfister with unusual, unreserved praise. When he first visited the secular, Austrian-Jewish Freud household, little Anna found his appearance so strange she thought he must come from another planet. Martin

Freud later recalled the time that he stumbled home, covered with blood, having been knifed in an anti-Semitic attack, and Oskar Pfister rose to his feet to shake Martin's hand, congratulating him on being wounded "in so just and noble a cause" [(1) p. 254]. Freud wrote of Pfister: ". . . he is a charming fellow who has won all our hearts, a warmhearted enthusiast, half Savior, half Pied Piper . . . ." Oskar Pfister Award winning Freud biographer, Peter Gay, wrote, "More than an ally to be used, Pfister was a companion to be enjoyed" and he quotes Freud's description of Pfister as "courageous, benevolent, honest" [(2) pp. 190-192]. Ernest Jones, who was there, wrote: "Freud was very fond of Pfister. He admired his high ethical standards, his unfailing altruism, and his optimism concerning human nature" [(4) p. 253].

Pfister, in turn, was not only a colleague, but an admirer. He described himself as ". . . dazzled by the beauty of that family life, which in spite of the almost superhuman greatness of the father of the house . . . breathed freedom and cheerfulness" [(3) p. 73].

Oskar Pfister was more than a trainee and guest of Freud. He was an important contributor to psychoanalysis, pastoral care, adolescent psychology, and the history of our time. Along with his original contributions to work with adolescents, he also wrote the first textbook of psychoanalysis, *The Psychoanalytic Method*, in 1913, translated into English in 1917. One of the first two lay analysts, Pfister's pursuit of psychoanalysis was an act of courage. In the years when Freud's ideas were considered absurd, disgusting, heretical and Jewish, Pfister endured years in danger of being defrocked and deprived of profession and income.

Freud tweaked Pfister, testing their relationship. But Pfister, manifesting his own vision of Christianity, could not be provoked, and he volleyed with the tease. It was in his correspondence with the Swiss clergyman that Freud made many of his wry, two-sidedly disparaging self-references. Freud called himself "a wicked pagan" and queried Pfister that, if psychoanalysis weren't antithetical to religion, ". . . why did none of the devout create psychoanalysis? Why did one have to wait for a completely God-less Jew?" [(2) p. 602]. Oskar Pfister replied that Jesus was the first psychoanalyst, but of Freud: "A better Christian never was." Freud insisted he was "an unrepentant heretic," and mused that the only thing Christian about him was the fact that he had been accused of being a "sexual Protestant!" [(4) p. 253].

Freud's contentiousness was more than humorous. Worried that Pfister was "over-decent" and might enlist psychoanalysis in the fight against sin"—while accepting Pfister's breakthrough into child analysis and expressing gratitude that psychoanalysis had been incorporated by a minister who worked with young and healthy people [(1) p. 254]—Freud wrote his pointed assault against religion with Pfister in mind. After writing his atheistic anthem "that had a good deal to do with Pfister," Freud then vacillated and delayed publication "in consideration of Pfister." Finally, Freud published *The Future of an Illusion* in 1927, expressing   ". . . my absolutely negative attitude toward religion, in every form and dilution . . ." [(2) p. 527].

How would the loyal disciple, who had risked his security for years to defend and promote psychoanalysis, respond when analysis turned its glare on him? He didn't accept: he didn't react. In the "Illusion of a Future," Pfister argued that religion inspires moral values and civilized productions; Peter Gay calls Pfister's prose "courteous, reasoned, most friendly" [(2) p. 536] and Freud found it "a kind reposte." Freud

had already praised Pfister's prose: ". . .
you write so gently, so humanely, so full of
considerateness, so objectively"—the very
tone Freud considered properly educative
[(4) p. 300].

Freud could be charmed, but not sedu-
ced. He wrote that regarding Pfister's view
of religion, "Our ways part at this point"
[(4) p. 343].

But Pfister, like a bronco-buster, could
not be shaken off. Earlier he had ridden out
prejudices and pressures, for, as Ernest
Jones wrote, "Very few gentiles withstood
the storm against psychoanalysis before
World War I," the exceptions being himself,
the great philosopher-analyst Binswanger,
Oberholtzer . . . and Pfister [(4) p. 357].
Pfister had also outlasted the break between
Freud and Jung (his old friend and co-
religionist), about which Pfister had written, "I have completely finished with the
Jungian manner, those high-falutin' inter-
pretations which proclaim every kind of
muck to be spiritual jam of the highest
order and try to smuggle a minor Apollo or
Christ into every corked-up little mind
simply will not do" [(3) p. 183].

Freud's children remembered that of all
the prominent men who paid homage to
their father, only Oskar Pfister always

showed interest in them, too. Almost unique among Freud's volatile friendships, the one with Pfister lasted until the end (in Jones' words) "without a cloud." Freud assailed Pfister's faith in humankind at the dawn of the Nazi era by writing to the clergyman: "I have found little that is 'good' about human beings. . . . In my experience most of them are trash." But Pfister, follower of prophets and foes of money-changers, mirrored to Freud his own high ideals.

Freud always addressed his letters to Pfister as "Dear Man of God." After reading about their friendship, I have come to realize that this was more than a taunt.

Numbered footnotes in this postscript refer to the following:

(1)   Clark, R. W. *Freud: The Man and the Cause*. New York: Random House, 1980.

(2)   Gay, Peter. *Freud: A Life for Our Time*. New York: Norton, 1988.

(3)   Donn, L. *Freud and Jung: Years of Friendship, Years of Loss*. New York: Scribner's, 1988.

(4)   Jones, Earnest. *The Life and Work of Sigmund Freud*. Edited in one volume by L. Trilling and S. Marcus. New York: Doubleday Anchor, 1963.

ACKNOWLEDGMENT

To my publisher, Sue Chance, for her enthusiasm, energy, and vision; and to the graphic artist we worked with, Deborah Bzdyl, for rendering our ideas in such a beautiful way. Thanks!